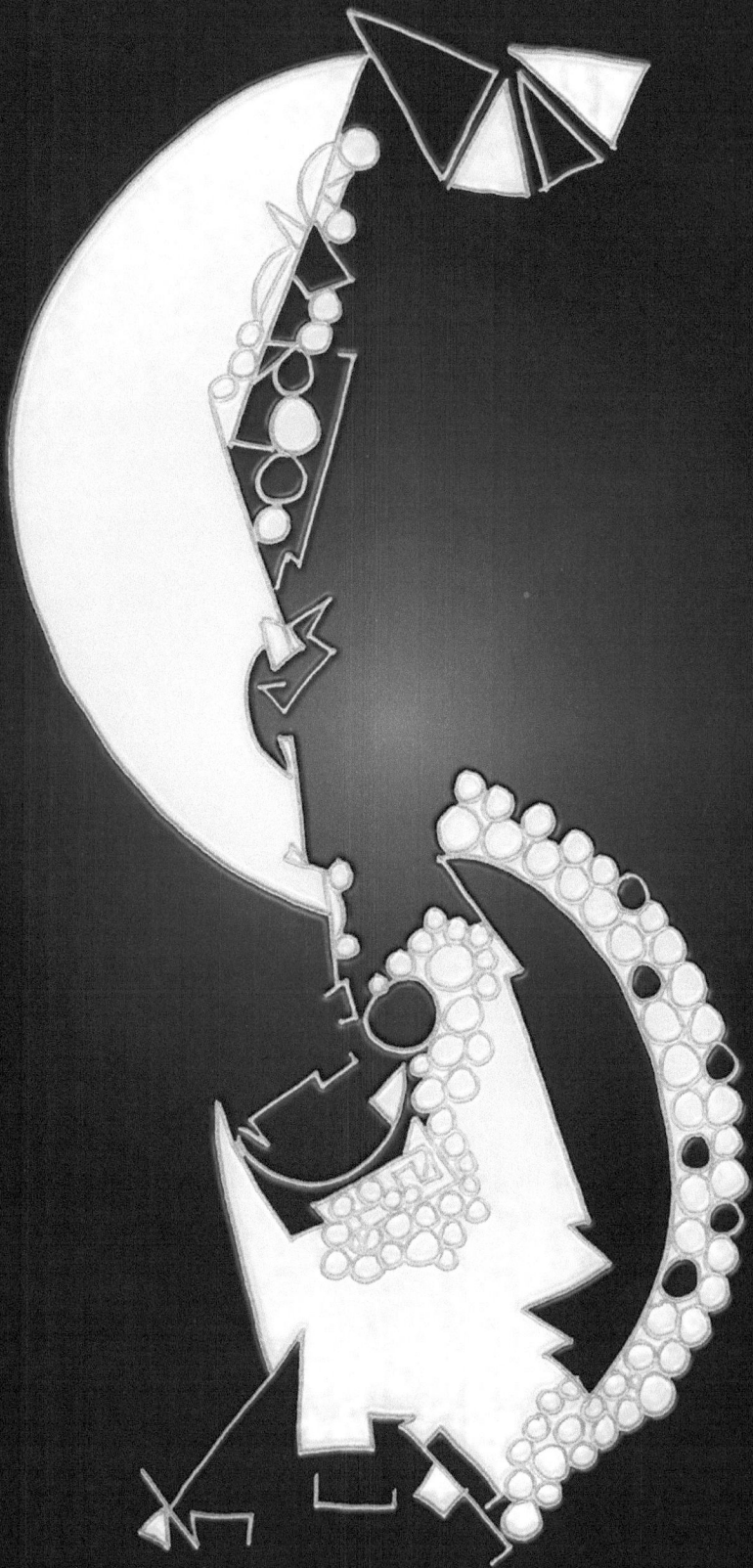

Golden Milk

Sheila E. Murphy

LBP

Luna Bisonte Prods
2020

Golden Milk

Some of the poems included in this
collection appeared in the following journals:

*Otata, Indefinite Space, Noon Anthology, Have your Chill,
Stride Magazine, Cruel Garters, Caliban Online, Zoomoozophone
Review, Descant, The Indianapolis Review, Clockwise Cat, Ginosko
Literary Journal, Coelacanth, Marsh Hawk Press, Synapse, Otoliths,
Abbey, Read On, Fell Swoop, experiential- experimental- literature,
Unlikely Stories, Word for Word, Black Sun Lit*

ISBN: 978-1-938521-64-5

Luna Bisonte Prods
137 Leland Ave.
Columbus OH 43214 USA

www.lulu.com/spotlight//lunabisonteprods

Table of Contents

Golden Milk

I'm lazy in the neck tonight, each starling mentions what I read
by hand, as syllables go dark against the backdrop tingling
mesh as if a signature made bold then faint then bold again

An effervescent fealty takes another name that threatens to
subtract sweetness from walled performance spaces meant for
pros and prose parlaying value for a venue meant to displace
pounce

Each earned inflection seems to curve into a place to be
affirmed I'm tired and ready to repeat an early
step to manufacture an inversion to be talked to death until
emergent wilderness comes through like a bank loan

I claim to love italics but in moderation, any time you walk
vocabulary words down lanes the empty sidelines shepherd
riverways where livestock and the sunlight chasten quietude

When at first I thought to cherish, sentences felt round again
and timed to mean a penny's worth of comfort for
a price no one afforded as maturity required infinity of
company

Winnowed by intention meaning breath the very current that I
draw for you to make a midnight half informal and recover
from the daylight forced into a place once honored now a sham
to ruin depth perception

The unevenness of Damocles equates to feeling frightened as a
patriarch who claims self-made ness where madness shows the
damages replay potential like
a phrase intoned by lesser minds

Now the brambles go to seed and singular displacement falters as the stories are retold retrieved and press ahead into the road lines leading one presumes to better placement where the lanes are blurred and scar

The riverways still carry thinking forward via bodies fresh from hammocks following the lie-down after winter engineered to formulate a sound distinct from tones once heard and rumored to subside

Who we each become as we together flow returns to teach us what we taught another else to tweak the words and silhouette a little melody with haloing from darkness hand knit scarves of light

This wash of young emotive bliss gives up restraint from flesh resembling dowager demeanor that would overturn the impulse to eject a rough and centered inference impossible to unfurl

The yield curve damages cardinal virtues in the balance makes us vestiges of thinking feeling breathing fluent light into another being until the boundaries dissolve become impossible to explain

Pirouette distills the body's innocence into a riveting advance to order the disorder and array new selves in tincture toward an exponential glee of leaving glyphs along the roadside and inventing new permission to be whole

Yes

Homophily detracts from shapely thought. A quiet history
comes back to taunt. Syllables when left alone show
goodness-of-fit. The tone of your remarks exasperates what
it exaggerates. The litmus shakes off center-stage
indenture. My home-fed darling, do you live the dreamscape
or abide by centered sight? *Lead me in your sleep.* Sorrow
folds itself in tidy squares until we wring our hands to
skeptical intention. Was it that way in our youth, regression
to the mean? My window is a syllable at least one time.
Finessing arteries implored to refuel depth.

Senators, then citizens, then no one there at all

Overgaard was lovely lace beneath

the sky's young face repeating

its eternity to washed space

between violets and minerals

untraced, the broken stalled

stovetops confirmed

smoothness woods and

glowing lines of kindling

to the tune of semiotic

staves a mile from obligation

trading wind for purity

of diamonds near the cloister

of the Eleanor the bread and blunder

speech of thought and motion

holding ground until the homonyms

went quiet echoing their last

I Used to Be a Person

I used to be a person I was interesting I used to be
and now I plod I plod through basic obligations
that shift constantly shift as if there were no stasis
The stasis I so love that tunes me to attunement

variegated and stilt free and maybe luminous
still luminous I used to want to dry out in the sand light
where the bathing suits were scarce and I could breeze
with all the sun breeze I could think I could feel

pulse your pulse I could be wooden or just flex
and I could read myself into the reeds and reading
and the dimples of the quasi light would beam
their tiny tidy little beamlets so the bounty was a thin

young overtone about to burst into a bluster
or a breast or even joyously foul language pretty
as a rap tone in the alley sunlight think about it
how can we still blush if there is only nothing there?

Wear Out Welcome

A gentleman of soft sweaters
and a mouth relaxed and listening.
What of the eyes would keepsake
what he heard?

The hands this graceful, that
forming a light grip on the arm rests.
Reported to build plots from scatterings.
Let them form themselves in range
of hearing. How he heard seemed quiet.

His photograph in black and white shows
gray with furniture and paneling.
A season disguised by being in the house.
We can guess by looking in on, just surmising
how the morning started and transcended into afternoon.

Just like that his visage held, and how it seemed
almost to know him was to want a talk
that would not come unless by accident.
If one began a conversation about something
he had noticed or had known then wished to say.

Brown Rice Green Tea

Give me a color to transcend, I'll drink to something
if you promise not to
give me something worse than joy to sip and savor and
savoy my way through down time

in the middle of faux Flagstaff woods and blooming
pine (does pine bloom) scents and sensing and serenity
all mine all ours all forenoon long and lengthwise
through the down time morning afternoon and frivolous

young incompletion I so love to bask in then report
then quiet down then freeze frame like eternity
should be comprised of all the scuttlebutt of nothing
to reveal report recuse recycle or rescind

I want my power of attorney to be lapsed and shadow
artistry if you still have a block of chalk a sidewalk
reminiscent of repairs nobody does or cares to do
have done or multiply into some farthing of a wall or cul-de-sac

Any Integer

To progress in life you must give up the things that you do not like.
- Agnes Martin

I have retrieved the tree that stays busy sprouting and then shedding leaves.

Successive and hinged features of what amounts to breathing as I know it.

Flecks of soft rain look like plump snow.

Any integer will do is how the caterwaul alerts us to nothing worth thinking.

I see my friend who is in pain at first now soften artificially as he relaxes into quiet.

I would prefer that he do work he learns to be.

Chapter includes versatile endowments. Plural things immerse us in them many days.

One moment is like this. It shifts.

We staple this to lean young branches at a time.

One sort of frost. The noise of January starting to recede into a pattern once let go.

I think there is robustness in ideas.

I tell them to a common mirror without seeking to accumulate.

I heard one fact or two be winter for a while.

Many pretty lines of code go wild again until smoothed down.

I need beauty to be there and multiply.

I need time to hold still.

If I evaporate, I need never notice.

Meaning might be tacit.

I watch you
Sleeping in a chair
The home sounds half alive
This early winter,
All mockingbirds gone still
And heat within the room
Soft on the skin.

You wake and ask a question
I can't answer. I try anyway.
You quiz me, and I know
How little I know
Despite a routine reflex
Lacking logic.

I learn to leave the room
Repeatedly, to keep myself
From being myself,
a source of sadness
in erosion.

And I dream the sky
I try to paint from memory and desire,
My hand brushing intuition
Quietly
I wish for energy
To retrieve what I have been.

14 Questions

1. What do you mean "Kick the tires?"

2. What if nothing we do in real life seems like poetry?

3. How many reeds does it take to learn to put away a woodwind?

4. If I offer you a deal, will you smother my sales speech?

5. Is there anyone who truly feels at home?

6. Why a priest (Is someone sick)?

7. Will I become my mother?

8. Whose integers are these and why are they infecting all my laundry?

9. What is the difference between a homonym and compassion?

10. Overall, would you say you gained from having lost your sense of direction?

11. What's the capital of lower case?

12. How many softballs does it take to make a home run?

13. Are you the one who came to the door last week selling onions?

14. Will you trade your confidence for this lightly used steel gate?

Meridian Street

Trees plush themselves into my viewfinder for now. Unless you're listening, become calm again. Your window anymore. The vault includes old depth as we envisioned who we were when driving past. Our line of sight rescinded energy as we maintained what we could gather once and then again. The salt in salary redeemed one person to another. How it was is who we were, we say again as photographs curl from the yellowed page. He was our father, and the color of the car was fast. Now every moment turns to morning. Fenders and young tire treads make their way across as if transcendence were yet possible.

Threads, threadbare, innocence, some cure

Three Untitled Haibun

He told me a poem was nothing but a peony. I said shut up
against my will. I said violets are always imprecise. He prayed
for slide rules. I looked that up on google, found few flaws.
There was desecration on the table where I placed my keys.
He told me noble facets of experience remove the need to make.
I said I wanted hunger to remove me. He was softer than emotion
when I looked into his eyes. Pale with winter any time. There
seemed this free zone far from voice. No matter what he said
I seemed to stay.

A harbor anymore, a fringe effect, the threads of little poses

*

I brought him from the neighborhood instead of staying home.
And now the white of where we were is chalked on fluently. He
speaks my language anymore. The updraft of insinuation loses
poise. We went one place and then another. Dancing seemed a
trace of what we knew from those we saw. I thought he was a
vision, then I talked back to no voice. We had in common what
we failed to leave where we had left. Sometimes I preach to who
I was along a calendar.

Breezeway, silhouettes of shadow, maybe relevance, perhaps just
noise

*

Alto voice meant sugar-coating on the dark wood of the library
where sheet music was held. Nothing to hear, nothing to sing,
only the faint smell of old volumes generally untouched. I thought
I heard a cat cross the deep floorboards, then I noted window
light a shade of true. There was the furniture, there were those
lapses of intelligence after the sadness that came flowing to the
fingerprints.

Slips of coming rain light near the glass, a thought before some
prompt for thin response

This

I cannot tell I am not
Thinking
As the butterfly resists
With powdery movement
The temptation to absorb
What it attracts

Time for Bed

Everything there is to know including everything I do not want to know pops up on my phone. Tomorrow's cloud light. I have already put wax earplugs in. Plan dreams I can't describe. Last night I tossed like romaine in a big glass bowl. I have an app that tells me how much restful, how much light. I have been thinking Issa, thinking Basho, thinking keyboard fluency amid avoidance of the rain. The muted alphabet, discernible through wax. How does one still pray? Memory differs from reasoning. Trees pruned allow in light I know by heart.

Unnumbered commandments, rationing of lockstep reflex, inventory

You Are the Better Fraction of Affection

Please do not forget you are the better fraction of affection
even when it's raining.
Please do not allow yourself to think that gray is real.
Gray is a symptom of amnesia for the sun.

Please remember that I love the halo that is always shining
as your life that hovers just above this life
that brings my life to light that is your light.
Remember how you light the very breath of living.

Please remember that gray is a mere fiction.
Rain forgets to shine and simply
splays across the streets and makes it hard to drive.
Remember you are vivid in imagination that is mine.

You are the better fraction of affection that resides in me.
Remember that a moment is as good as
the eternity we're promised every day
by someone we cannot hear well enough.

You are the sunlight and the homonym of joy
that lives across my life, and I beseech you:
Hear yourself continually blossoming along my heart.
Do not forget you are the better fraction of affection.

The Chivalrous Relay of Puce

Against a patchwork quill penumbra
leave the world to Jennifer
my coin friend in the summer
of detritus when your indigo is small

as spawned as generosity itself
alongside window dressing
sturdily confessed astride the moonscape
and its glinty afterthought

full on as warded off the cuff
in the domain of angst you brothered
prior to the seen salacious purposeful
detente made willful as a chemist

on the fly still needling the spittoon's museum
quality Magnificat whole hog
as pebbles waste the spun sun
spattering neglected raindrops

Friday Night in a Falsetto Portugal

Whose Labrador is your good work
amid the spritzed petunias on a continent
halfway around affordability and chores?

Are you glistening as I recite my innocence?

Anymore the dowry is an artifact chewed into by intention.

Delirium effaces reeds and cloth and pointillist detente.

Primary-recency fits Chicago like a furnished glove.

Matchmaking in general has ceased to be a sport
in heaven; for the nonce, reading has come
to seem an innovation as the eyes all close in unison.

Turn to One

He felt the several of them turn to one. A mother.
Light toward his breath. His forehead smoothed as though
no winter. Mild eye light amid an always afternoon. Within
the room he was a boy lost in the sweet wheel of how a
moment stays. Where only one is there with him, her place.
This effort and this effortless completeness. How the world
without a name remains.

Language, miniature mind fall, open heaven, closed
to proof

She Divests

The home once handsome seemed a crafted color, shaped
pieces that had formed a life. Now elegance gone quiet has
divided her attention. Her seeing distances the breath from
how the leisure once was felt. A shade of white blue
tempering glass frost. Some lines turned two-dimensional.
The way the neighbors who arrive one at a time seem
singular, then leave again. She looks toward a corner from
her place within the room. As though retrieving it from
history, sans recollection. Just the haze of daylight in a pale
relief.

Clasped hands, halo projected to another side, some wants

Tidy as a Globe

She leaves him in her heart. He freshly goes away.
She windows her relief apart from speaking. How it was,
now shallow in her mind looking away. He centered, and he
fell, and now a foreign sun comes home through doorways
she has framed. A way of softening the dark breath comes.
She pieces conversation from her mind to form another
portrait she might call a self. With thin supply of paint, she
anchors what was there. By way of limited biography, tidy
as a globe. Were the world he gave her safe, he might have
cried, that she might trust a future time.

Petals littered on the walkway, tiny wind, desire to
walk again

Already Now

The transplant has already taken place. My place is
portable; the lift, risen without me. And potential turns to
vine that finds ascent. I look out across the red rock and
find the full moon centering each story. What will be will
brace itself and we will acquiesce, say lines that lead to
other lines. I try rehearsing to prelude performance, but the
rise in decibels takes hold. I dry my hands now often
washed of you. Is there a moment in the future I can catch?
The lamp echoes thin moonlight. As my skin reflects a
history of sun.

Gem stones, paths the color clay, walkways

No text

No call

18,844 steps

When I Quiet I Am Not Who I Become

The leaves of these vast summers do not mulch, for oak is poison to the ground.

My mother calculates the number of labor hours it takes to rake them to the street.

I come home from school and I keep going back, and I keep coming home.

The wind has smoke.

I think a cup of tea.

Of all the paint strokes Mr. Richardson put down across the white face of the house before the leaves began to fall.

I heard him speak I stood there asking things and he responded from the ladder top.

Now all day I listen and I orchestrate the conversation, stir the different syllables.

Can you be quiet as the house attracts its color?

I look around the inside walls of quite another home in which adulthood was supposed to happen.

How is this familiar when I'm busy being young?

When I imagine I am learning.

The sky is full of flutes at rest, I know them better than I know the leaves before they fall.

I think the glassed-in home I had at first allowed my eyes to close.

Nurse Molnar at St. Joseph's Hospital in Mishawaka, Indiana.

I could open them to those who wanted me to last.

Portrait

She was lovely as a lily for a while, then found a place to sleep she liked better than sunlight. Dreamed darkness endowed with cursive thought. Outside, mist caressed the greens. A willow took in breeze. She turned to a memento of her former self. Her thought became the body, and her body held its place. The elements learned to feel for her. She left hope on the table, and her breathing shifted. Anymore, the garden lifted, and whatever rain would rinse its way.

Apartness as a rule, contrivance or a natural release

Capsicum you said. All right. I breathe in what you
breathe out and say yes (again). Take this
and I will offer that.
We have arrived at what I thought

I might resist yet knew
today was always
viable. This model. This blue
line of sky. This wide vehicle

transporting us to names of places
I don't care what they are named.
I only watch you form
another mirror full of me.

I stay the course I made I think
you know that practice
that defines me overtime.
Just like the partial view I gave you of my destiny.

Stars harsh with shine elapse
into my hunger for a quiet day
to night span. In a moment
I will be a rose inside my brain pan.
Silently alert, alone to you,
I will your voice unto the willing
where a lifeline lapses anymore.
The white behind the penmanship
grows tall. And we are meant to be
entwined I hear myself declare.
Because it's spring again and all
the shadows pause for silk.
They milk their way out of my happiness.
I pick flowers. I rescind what I gave freely.
Now there's no one to reclaim
what I give up. I give up haste
and find a little pacem, honoring
Pope John from child days.
How cool monastic feeling seems
a season between symphonies
through which my alto rises to achieve
its point of tensing when I speak to you
the way I used to do when we were trembling.

He Built

He built me a window like a prince. Grammar voices
me again. I thought it might be consummate to wield
a kitchen in plain view. Who's hungry? Kismet falsified
already impeded records. Breath works this way: voice
minus voices minus now. In a hoodwinked kind of way, I
think I'm milder than your progeny. Who knows winter
biblically? The frost revokes our privilege anymore. And I
am fostering a prize bull here in this slim pen. The only
conversation feels like rumor, and detail are flittering from
yeast to bells and whistles. I would like to show my hand if
there were scores behind it. Altercations make us bristle,
and the fewer, the more rescue.

Consequential seasons, seasoning amid a plain containment,
strides and strip malls

I Think You Know Where This is Going

Darkness means a pool of missing light.
As recess looms, the dream begins to taste of spritz
those secrets hollowed out of moons
and surfaces that size the waves
of music caught in someone's reflex
like the segment of a line
I think you know where this is going
as the fog begins to follow
how it was Europe our young heart
full of music tinned from cheap flutes
leaving weather at the zero point
in time to show what cabbage means
to children coded out of privacy reflecting
the silk sleep of reason
in the city nicknamed urgency
one huge island stands and whispers chill
along an argument with answers to retract
some of the breathing that churns twelve tones
left beautiful as they were when channeled
near the vacancy signs plucked from ground
when witnesses repeated fragile lapses in recall
as sculptures perished intention
and blame revealed the finish line
projected then ignored
truth often overstays its welcome
kindling lack of interest in the unfamiliar pockets
emptied long ago when blandishments would linger
in the autumn air of Flagstaff where we were

Truce

fervor loosens the weave
sweet soft arms clothed
in gentle threads of wool
made white from bleach

the land in parallel
achieves a peace
and many nights concede
to the intelligence

of leitmotif made thin
as ice yet warm
the small lane near
a pasture wide

and lavished with
inflection that means
avenues are poised
toward destinations combed

Chair

Look at the wood painted blue
kisses on both cheeks
a rabble roused inflection
spawns delinquent splash

of glitz and same
in equal measure
stilted tones to mime
intention coiled around an absent center

never enough windows
to invent transparency
only a word unpolished,
unconfirmed, withdrawn

and still in costume
throughout the hours of daylight
turned to frost and dusk
until accentual contentment frames the rest

Clyfford Still

Why yellow here
Why blood black
I just heard breath go new
In this aroma near sparks that sustain
I dry my hands of all your paint
The scant young semaphore still faint
I blush into the woodwinds I would play
Were it not for you and death and parity

In Season

Brandish spokes of light you claim to have invented in your spare time. Take these herbs and toss them in your tea. A homily the cat is used to hearing fades as the monsoon seeps in. Once-scrubbed windows now defined by streaks define July. Is there a chaplain in the house? Stamens capture the attention, and the moon sounds dry. Age revokes some privileges in favor of just listening. As opinion saturates what once seemed dry.

Mid stacks, the powdery scent of scholarship and quiet

This Humidity

Together, we design a speaking part for God
reflexively ignored by the nominal base.

Everyday hemp hastens predicted softness
one is tempted to perform, preformed.

The therapist hovers on the threshold
of releasing patients one after the next.

Angst remains contagious as a language
linking neighbor to very neighborly denizens.

Indices intended to reveal truth participate
in a cost-benefit analysis of philosophy.

Is there any reason to be loved again?
And if so, at what level of granularity?

For Summer

If ever I am
warm again, consider
your performance role.
in which the subject predicates

recasting sky light
wedged between
rooftop and
imaginary singing,

blemishing the other-
wise mishandling
mangled psycho-
logical foray into

invention forged into
a white stone fact
of swamp
life rigor mort.

Yet

Scapular retracts
the sin not yet
committed as
forgiven once

the shelf life hastens
to regard a wash
a signature retention
of the once recruited

pale cadets gone
singular onto the pathway
littered with repeat signs
posing as diverse as if

to think equaled in kind
rapport the fingering
for F# above
familiar middle-C.

Hypothesis

Fears poured into
thimbles or cauldrons
might produce,
evoke no value

within earshot
lingering beyond
bedpost the
rumored bed rest

safety or satiety
turned godly
overtones placed
under wash lines

where birds
hold still
unlike us, rattling
along the panic line.

The Long Drive Toward Self Actual

Paradise eludes erasure. Lives in me. Contentment takes
a breath(er). I divest my present tense of sight. Release the
pressure of intent. Seen my id of late? I used to think it was
divisible. I used to think. The long drive toward self-actual fell
to depths. I now revoke what privilege I had thought. Look
forward for the backdrop once recovered from a jest. Are
we within hearing? Semaphore is fact, as are indelible
arrangements of what was and will be with me always.
How to describe the one-off self, left on a shelf without
intention.

Elastic soul, the bandage covering the theory of rendition

Venture

You take my arm, we go another where. How might moonlight
seem a transit to another sky? We clothe ourselves in stars.
The only trial heaven is this flight. Toward charm the center-
fold, each question not in view. Trims tones and sharpens
slight behaviors. Each waking syllable sounds in my skin.

Telling something, featherish dimension, salt released
from wounds, good night

Holdings

Let the professor train the ear to find finality in stingy eighth
notes for a time. Pale holdings come to this: the mantra is
indelible. My store home, plain. The many windows
proclaimed face far away. And now the clock has ticked
enough, she says, and thus the loud truck comes to pay
respects. A daylight logged in place. People arrive, and they
replay the works.

Daytime anymore, the golden and the night light frosting
passages of snow

Please

Be my finishing school, my jovial run-of-the-mill Millennial.
A trinity of unrequited samples gifts me back to earth. Come
long with me, come sprint through feckless decades of old
wilt. The thunder hastens to revive some selves projected
on our own. Love lessons reveal that any spring is possible
when no one's on the take.

Elastic mood, the selvedge, syllables tossed in for grins

Interval

How many decibels does it take to finish hosting drama now? Is now a mere pastime? In dust or acrimonious new takes on what was then? When I was young just yesterday, I carved today. I craved what I might be (again) or any time a tall. The cinders made their tones and I considered that percussion. Waves and drainage and commodities as if contained. The minister of miniscule endorsements feigning typecast acumen.

Good sport, waffling, definitive decisions lingering in middle distance

Patience at the Fence

Always I overhear the overbearing neighbors fail to wince
where I would fall back on my store of tiptoe. Radical
displays of lariats and stem cells in the embassy. Integers
and tatting and roan haste. The high school annual is in the
basement where the husbands are. Apprentices look wary
and why not? Whoever shames her twin shall splinter
mirrors showing twelve long stems. Rulers leak intervals
when no one looks. Continuo means too much work. The
breaststroke glistens in chlorine. A tacit plastic sheeting
along pool top. To smother telltale plots. The livestock
populate each story while the new monks pray.

Desolations, sample size, the rose lined avenue at dusk

On Pause

Noon grows back like tissue still obedient to code in fibers of
successive recollections. As flesh and blood relapses into a
routine. The motion sensor aspirates until no weather outside
selves seems palpable. Infallible momentum strikes a chord
and population numbers spawn the act of chance as the design
of leaves that color and come down to shift the earth into a
host of new beginnings.

Sample size, the simple act of being seen beyond the seen

Now

I watch her lose the word for *vinegar*. The clothes are clean. A glow about the yard, soft morning after yet another morning. All the world is speech without vocabulary. I hear her reach across to touch a thing she seeks. I say a name. The walls, pure white, or close. And that rectangular window, very like the painting. With the sound of hurt, from reach, as sleep that does not come. How can I paint the closeness now? How do the sounds ascend to where we were and who we are again?

Northerly

She minimized her way toward
the cusp of lottery and satisfice.
All daylight lofty sinecure showed
damage after loss confined to tentative
restraint from altar cloths and silver water
shattering the unmasked safety of a toss-up
between brazen haste and stall.
Now warm ventures shrill beneath
salt light and body chemistry aligned
with white waved flags mean
one chapter or another has elapsed
to memory unlatched until the craft
weighs heavily on land before we cross.

See Whether

Ask her if
She notices
The big blue shadow
Change the look of moon

The anyold
Space between
Now and then
Now and again

November

I used to like to up-front differences
To iron them out
Now I've given that away
To cut my losses

On the sole melody we had in common versus
New harmonic breath
We catch, release, allow
To get away.

Love is less impossible
When I consign myself
To peace instead
Of smoothing wrongs.

How is it possible the sky
Can shine across the river
Anymore, the heart beat
Purely as the distance from a grave?

Pencil

Lead is soft
Page is soft
I write something
You may read

Another city
Full of windows
Means paintings
In the many minds

I practice being
Quiet by myself
With you away
From here

I hear speech
Invisible I indulge
In your language
Invincible

This New Year

White trees, smooth lake, pale stars.

Recall the moment in your life
when you felt most loved,
that allows your mind to honor
its companion heart.

The crunch of steps across
a deepened surface of new snow
forms little histories
to embellish or relate,

in a world replete
with accidental miracles
that reveal for each of us
a reason to belong.

Singing in the Dead

I far prefer the kinder to be home. Their masks are wood,
their eyes are blond. The squawk of paint removes a
threaded vetting of contiguous *marchons* until the ladder
dries (viaticals still vie). A mother lode is fickle while the
thickets phase out vines.

We undermine our caveats once verisimilitude catches.
Fireflies anoint their prey. Let us divine our way through
penitence. (Someone forgive my innocence.)

Repay me my altercations as I forgive those who spin
control out of my captions. Limit me Lord, only by my
salter. I convene this group of heretics for purposes
unknown.

Myopic referenda stop the QB from advancing. Ruminative
theory blanches the already white lines on the field. A color
code repurposes the fealty of the line coach.

Obfuscation can be fundamental obvious. Whose nest
is this anyway? The curse of Reuben sandwich is the cube of
salt not there.

Weeds violate the din of offset prose. You vintage me.
I forewarn. You rattle your own cage replete with rage.

At this moment's notice, elected shepherds drive the wrong
flock in the wrong direction

A New Routine

Resume vivace. Find the cup
To ripen space. Alleviate,
Revive. Untie the stitched
Warped to weakness.

Maybe anybody busy
Hurtling toward the unplanned
Finish line evaporates intact.
Who knows who cares?

Dominoes reputed to effect
Downturn may be rumors
Only skittled in a curve
Not named. Apply your name?

How do you want to be
Recalled, if at all?
For slumber, or no waves,
For thick vast summer sprawl?

Now That

Now that I have something
I have something to protect.

This unwoven world may own
moments in common or may not.

How do we connect when we do not
resemble? How might we derive a lesson

from a lesson not yet learned?
The earning of a heart refashions

something of a brain, an engine particled
into invisible détente allowed in keeping.

As the moment freshens to another moment,
how will we remember what we thought?

And will it matter anymore? Will this point of thinking
translate to another place from which to start?

We Agree More than We Disagree

To pivot is an art
formatted by the body
chemistry poised
to make shifts hasten.

Are you listening
or merely gravitating
back to zero
read of the odometer?

Mood swings demean
soft spelling bees
where photo likeness
breeds consent.

A mere pro forma,
this debate team oxymoron.
versus meeting up after to decide
who got it wrong.

Tonight

You were paging through the Harvard scrapbook fingering
the letters Artis wrote on onion skin typed on both sides
including pencil drawings of a place. Planning times to meet.
In those days people missed each other as addresses
changed and most affection came by stamps some weeks
beyond their rendering. You spoke of missing what was
meant beneath those letters on the page, the difficulty
reading, the responsibility for teaching so well the children
wept the moment that they learned that you would leave.
How do you retrieve a moment missed the first time?
Innocence breeds honesty you can't get back or give. The
moment owns humidity sometimes. Gray clouds protect. We
try to keep up with the tiny history we float against
imagination if it's there. How many signatures does it take
to integrate one conversation to remain for life?

Moments ago, the absence of invention, tabled time

Breath of Her

She speaks fragrance that shifts
a kind of hunger in the eyesight that beholds her.
Sostenuto, this late in the day,
a forest of shared heart.

Sustaining moisture as the sky
empties its white,
releases an emotive stance.
We live together in the warmth

of a perfume we have invented
out of habit. And the night
forthcomes as we repeat
respective daylights.

As though winter were a tall
imagined brevity just vertical,
not lasting at all,
as life we elevate eventually goes small.

Logic Makes Me Tired Again

Caught between the impulse to convene a quorum
and desire to frame self-portraits in composite,
I gentle past the stream of thought that narrows taut robustness
to a clamp.

Now we know the furtive looks amount to something
primitive or stolid or refractive.
Why not loop new sensibilities with straight-edged lines?
The mauve in anybody's eye light stains each future.

Now we warm our toes beside the fictive flame light
as we sample autumn in its time
when nursing one sweet candle of the dream,
showing how slowly we absorb our little lives.

How many if-then seeming nautilus extractions
minnow toward our here-and-now without the prompting
we are used to? Many instances of water
dousing flame and shrill lamé a moth away from paradise.

Somewhere around coffee sun the air
Perfects the inbreath of the solitude

Innocence

I take back the statement that provoked you
pulling out your hair
within the margins of my lifeline.
My empathy is killing someone else.

If you don't recognize the pattern,
raise your index finger
to confirm I hear you to my face.
I feel unsure what moves I ought to make

to take a stand. If there is silver
near the plate, then take it back
to where you came from.
Coping is for wizards, not for saints.

Miracles reveal how routine lives
convey an instance of sobriety.
As you capsulize this message,
why am I not looking in your mirror?

It keeps trying to be Lent,
and I am very young again.
The leisure premise of my dog walk
(and I have no dog) means active voice

where I have tabled my intention.
Left to whose devices must we nomad
more than depth allows?
Pearl necklaces might quirk us out of townhomes,

or repair our lives still premised on
convivial restraint. I want a descant
to come true and homonym my
life's work. Anyway, the obstacles

included in my course mean spring
has shafted the ID cards shown
that kindle a relationship with God
or anybody named as co-conspirator.

I Promise Gentleness

I promise gentleness will lead you back
to where you will recall
beginning.

The women you are hearing now remind you
what you never said
but will.

An easy way to forward what you dreamed
is to decide today is that
and claim.

How perfectly your purity imagined turned to flesh
how noticeable
now.

If ever you are quiet then the circumstances will
speak back the lack
of separation.

Some People

Some people know people
while others do not
They look on wondering
how a thing begins.

There seems so little chemistry,
so many windows draped shut
No one starts up something, and yet
people speak to other people.

And the friendships seem like
movies that you watch and think
you might be in one day,
then days pass into other days.

And you are still apart from
all the people who know people
and they don't know you
you don't know them.

Imagine

Imagine being happy with your name
splayed large across each windshield
each billboard each figurative
once blank space

Your name your face everywhere
there is to look your name
your face your words
the rasp of speech in spurts

And everyone assaulted with the sound
of syllables repeated hammered across windshields
spattered onto space nothing to come of it
just raw spewing of dross

No thought of quiet no place to rest
no mention of a still point
around which all the spin continues
not a whit of silence not a moment not a breath

Nerves

The word *nervous*
seems quaint today.
Practically no one
says *I'm nervous.*

We had a neighbor,
a little boy, who cried,
You nervous me!
His mother was shrill.

You could feel
the very word
wear down his spirit,
hurt the skin.

My skin has held
years of nerves.
I need a rest from
pretending them away.

Late

Talk to me slowly as warm milk.

I hear only a candle seep into the soft night.

And beyond, these fixtures of recall fill out the picture anymore.

The guesses of July preside over the lawn and walkways.

A very white young evening has elapsed.

Again a name, a word, the feeling of an incremental darkness.

Reflex

She decided she would not
disturb his sleep.
His insomnia reduced her
range of motion.

Curtains fell closed
against late night
and prevailed
amid the early light.

A story sheds its path
until repeating it
confirms a way
to hear.

Any day now, she or he
mused to self.
As all the days so far resembled
all those they had known.

Ovation for the Overtones

Stand down, Baltic Bill. Allow my evanescence to retrieve what you were looking for beneath the down quilt. Humor me, my boy. It's teacup midnight, and the lashing rain slaps windows under my hand made duress. To truthify this instant, buy a comma or wainscoting to form pause points just around the corner from garage after garage. I think I'm finished siphoning the relics from the dross, so come by when you're finished playing charades with elders on the porch. It's mealtime in the Arctic now, so blunder on with how you think you think and teach me to pretend to hear. Your honor is a field day for the ladies chirping rodeo abandoned grace notes. Whinnying between goalposts measured by the shared recall.

Sanctify

This prayer is not your prayer. It is an adjective. A breath. A substance already abused. An integer to carve up and distribute to the 1%. It is an interval. A post-op, post-doc, postulant for keeps. It is a magnifying grasp of fate.

This prayer is obvious to a statistician. It is at the breaking point about to earn its hundred thousandth citation. It is gorgeous at the core when no one's listening.

This prayer aspires to be a shepherd in the middle of the city when it's dark. It is a portion of the maverick's estate. It is a symphony of chalk marks left in the odometer's will. It is a clockface bruised by truth.

This prayer comes in a four pack as consumable as treacle. It is thick in shared experience and pocked. It is a kind of crucifix in process. It is furred and wet and thought-free. It is damaged by the weather still rehearsing. It is depth still unperceived.

Pantoum for Autumn

The lonely ones arrive and do not leave.
Listen to pond light carry stages of deflection.
I think I am mimetically in love.
Against the grain go dove tones from past lives.

Listen to pond light carry stages of deflection.
When an opening arrives, be sure to ping a candidate.
Against the grain go dove tones from past lives.
Professors emeriti hold fast to offices and documents.

When an opening arrives, be sure to ping a candidate.
Photosynthesis reveals new hope for the faithful.
Professors emeriti hold fast to offices and documents.
A hall pass may have seemed my fondest wish.

Photosynthesis reveals new hope for the faithful.
What kind of feather floats from a mid-level branch?
A hall pass may have seemed my fondest wish.
One daylight not the same as any other.

What kind of feather floats from a mid-level branch?
The power of reasoning leaves many wanting.
One daylight not the same as any other.
Optimize the granular experience before it fades.

The power of reasoning leaves many wanting

Metrics taste of virgin olive oil.

Optimize the granular experience before it fades.

The Amalfi Coast reflects an inner warmth.

Metrics taste of virgin olive oil.

Rapport descends to factual material.

The Amalfi Coast reflects an inner warmth.

How can a Lazy Susan match rotating crops?

Rapport descends to factual material.

I think I am mimetically in love.

How can a Lazy Susan match rotating crops?

The lonely ones arrive and do not leave.

Ninepins for July

1/

That year, he said something somebody wrote down; it has been quoted ever since. It was a simple thing deflecting an assumption that he was a certain kind of being. He informed the inquisitor that this did not feel true.

2/

An avid lover of olive trees can look with interest at a white grape-hued hard tiny fruit upon a brick pathway. This might have been a candidate for something to be pickled in a jar and shoved into a truck somewhere before being sold virtually next door.

3/

The emphasis of a given homily was on some six hundred rules that turned into a festival of hall monitors who would call attention to mistakes performed by others, thereby lessening the time for finding love.

4/

She spent acres of time sorting the contents of six boxes of possessions that belonged to offspring, that each ingredient might be placed on a particular shelf and left again.

5/

The argument resulted in a standoff that occupied the mind of one of the combatants who hoped for health and ease to come back to the spirit and the flesh.

6/

He wrote a postcard including more than anyone would want to know yet furnishing enough to make sure things had left his chest.

7/

To celebrate alternative dependence, people found their way to lighters that would yield successive pops that lit the sky, that there might form a relaxation around the caged mentality that now prevailed.

8/

The therapist arrived with tools of her trade that she might rescue someone from intended peace and spawn confusion in an otherwise pale home.

9/

Present tense replete with derivations spawned a missing of the point as new pasts gathered in pursuit of future design attributed to informal survival.

In Situ

Fluency condones
the expert witness of the heart
wedged between bruises
formed of fact,
meshing the passion with the ivy.

Solo bowls replete with green opinions
yield to *yonge sonne*
lighting the fairgrounds
whose innocence, still undiscussed,
is closing in on circumstantial penitence,

the blond leafing through blinds
with magnified indentured
ways and means
advancing through the embers
of the damned.

Sentences and Saplings

Major winter dry tails languish in the seasoned headwinds / furry
as a chore. I take my cue from tall doors to be frogmarched through
the wormwood fractions of indecency.

Unparsed ovations manage traction sounding half contagious.
Many infancies retract inverted history.
For now the altar feels like cloth without a table.

What would a reunion of the charities be like amid dark stalks of rain
porching the tidy histories of place light:
Auckland, Darwin, Cleveland, Banff,

pathways from here and veering toward insomnia for hire.
The fractions gravitate to mismatched parts and summer near
the caterwaul of dime-a-doz repressions.

Center me against the lovely weeds and comrades earning copacetic
intuition plucked out of the want ads from another time
of marathons, embroidery, and captions lifted from the always west.

Matins

She introduced the topic *listening*. For a moment all the mockingbirds retreated to the wire where they were lubricating separate melodies. I had to sort. I needed to reciprocate. So many birds singing in thirds. Distinct from speech conforming to an interrogative lilt. A senior leader told de facto children they would not be hired if they insisted on intoning weakness and uncertainty. I listen to her feather dust the garden of the many webs. Cool morning raptures of some lines of code that must be music. Every fleck of maturation leads to song. I would absorb even the window light if it were true.

Ghazal for Here

Op cit's from the Galatians baby, let the pastor go.
For lamentation's breathy trill and middle age is slow.

Dapper gents are dime a doz' and wicked boring low.
Better take the plunge to find a glistening young doe.

Tempt cash out of the register and let your feelings glow
Let winter pass and lose the gloves and tender what you sow.

Swirl through totem taciturn authorities in tow.
And give yourself some wiggle room and hit the old dance flo'.

Eternity's a big blue bag of epicentral flow.
So get your moxie flowering, put on a gorgeous show.

Be quick to cue temptation, bring it on right in a row
Allure the mirror images to come transcend each beau.

Transubstantiate the outtakes, chafe the status quo
Align again with wilderness amass the art of glow.

Weather Sestina

It's time the cat came in from weather.
We earn our happiness behind closed doors.
A rectangle of a flashing story holds our eyes.
I stay in the mood to watch you watch
uneven spatters of storied deception
we summarily hash out again.

Everything we do we plan to do again
within the confines of this monsoon weather.
Despite predictions, we agree there is deception
by authorities who function behind doors.
We pretend them out of thinking as we watch
the evolution of a story in their eyes.

No matter what emerges from twinned pairs of eyes,
people who know declare we will repair again
to safety where the planets are available to watch.
But viewing differs under every weather.
We tell ourselves we are protected by the doors,
to keep from falling prey to a deception.

I know how weather people are with water, a deception
rimmed around their darting eyes.
If only there were open doors
to foster coming in and going out again
to find agreement about weather
and help us form decision trees to watch.

Once we have called the cat, then we can watch
what neighbors do to maintain the deception
of predictability in weather
that begins to bring out allergies in eyes.
We go through rituals and Kleenex again,
making sure to close the windows and the doors.

Whose idea was it to buy French doors?
Now we have agreed we have to watch
the traffic and sidewalks again
to keep out the deception,
verify the safety with our own eyes
as the desert serves us weather.

For now, we must avert all semblance of deception.
It is not enough simply to watch
amid this variable and seasoned weather.

Closeness

Those within a radius of thinking distance stood no chance.
He preferred to melt into relationships that looked good in
print. Does anybody really know these people? Solitude
meets silence in the corridor then nods and walks on. He is
in general too good for present tense. Friendship manifests
itself before an audience. He wants to broadcast what that is
to those he would not choose. As is a cumulative way to
seek becoming, to acquire. His vintage thus replete with
choice and taste in reputation.

Tacit refusal of the blooms along the walkway and the
breaths between

I reify your doubt by way of code

the mother lode of onus on us

situationally vague as syllables

thought spot on and sipped sideways

Your Handsome Innocence Thus Resurrected

I picture touch
I breathe in sound
I recognize the difference between
you and not you.

Anymore the daffodils and white sand
coalesce.
And equally, small coats around the tiny stars protect
sweet light.

I reason with my sense and skin,
your eye light's unexpected peace
toward land to cross
beneath new sky.

Why explain
the leaflets when the leaves transcend,
the small thin path beyond
some hypothetical grand plan?

You Are Not from Here

I wish you uniform coordinates, the lark light of a morning,
a seeping season early green. Close reading the cloister of
intention. As impending isolation follows full immersion in
community. To crouch beside a plant to weed away the
lamentations that crowd freshness. Lily wise inflection of
firm petals and immunity to rain.

Curvature in boundaries, meticulous young color free
to vary amid risk

One Moment in July

I did not argue him away from his affection. I left off thought
and let it be awhile, this arduous July of heat and friction
and desire for coolness if some smoothing could evolve.

He was asking my agreement, and my voice relaxed
into professional response, conveying maybe
that opinions matter less than what we build between us,

part intentional and part an accident in openness.
How is everyone important independently? The space between
one voice and another cradles something in us wanting

to be played the way a violin or game of handball might,
with every facet of being intertwined with
every facet of being known and almost loved.

Because that's what we do when we allow the softness
spirited and clear and gentling toward a picture
that includes the roses and the nutrients and land and breath and sky.

Tough as Teak

You prince me anymore.
I fold or not.
Is this the nascent hibiscus
I am thinking to replace the rose of old?

Maybe you don't know
the list of things I do not
know. Remember is the byword
as an evening gradually unevens

how our daylight went
once we were sold
on the idea of a lance
to factor into how

one vaults across experience
in that quasi way of saying
half of what we mean,
then look askance.

Midnight Sunshine

Tell me a story, and I'll chaperone your lies.
Make sentences as sparse as desert rain.
I'll record your every breath mark that inclines to words
to capture as if stains on spaces of these staves.

When you sing words, remind them
to connect. Just as an insistent darkness
may trespass on the dusk as if to quell
lark tunes that reverberate escape.

Bring home the state of who we were
as we held still within this place
we did not make or name, but lived
resisting any urge to shift away.

And now the dovetailing of lifelines
capture what an innocent might believe
amid the rubble and the rumors
and the lines laced into fiction to adore.

You Have a Habit of Not Being

Perfect. Let's start there. The
source of my desire
and admiration.

A gray window changes
nothing other than
my impression.

Is solipsism legal here?

I hear commencement
happens later in the month.
When all the bells turn whistles.

Very many posses taking
shape and selfies with
importances so deemed,

as if all local color
were not color anymore.

I Am Sorry I Do Not Write Back

He told me as we stood masked along the north street side
he is depressed more than before. I tell him
the same without the words I listen to his eyes.
I watch him shift the mask it's difficult to breathe,
yes, it is quiet near the sanity that we presume
to hold and then retrieve and lose again.

How are we neighbors anymore, how were we then?
What is the meaning of deciduous, my lonely perfect friend?
Why are we defined by what we barely can describe?
The weather taints the skin, the street is full of gray,
he told me he has lost so many decibels and pounds.
I am in touch with hunger, I dispose of
all the symptoms.

We have many things to talk about, we are confounded by
purported leadership synonymous with lust.
The world is just a little round, the world is not communicable.
We thought we had it nailed and now the fingerings
have been forgotten, and the tones are long
and broken, and then breathed so many times, like bodies
we believed we owned or were, that only hold a little while.

This, Too

Trace a rook from tall to keeling
Thirst, our vastness leans to veritas.
Clasp a lie then strut.
Whose britches glow with kissing.
Flow, flow, hen that spans a multiplicity of flings.
Drop sighs.
Sows can span a myriad of strings
Once plucked, fill up
With stakes in rollick
As the few who dwell
will tarry across creeds.

Simulacrum

"It was evening all afternoon."
William Carlos Williams

Now before I bathe, I dry.
Temptation lunatics its way south
Where I writhe to seam the limbs near peace
I pray to weather
Just as we do now.

Remake my vortices until I cry
The depths within you, notice
There are syllables to wring from threadbare
Sentiment I graze to breathe
From scratch. Why don't you

Memorize my laundry and come clean.
The drapes are taut with fiberglass,
And I each fleck of cloth can break
The way skin emulates results
Of an election where nobody tithed.

You Are the Magnolia

You are the magnolia and I dream impetuous trespass
where few roads converge mid woods.

We halfway occupy these bodies choiced to transcend
destinations fragrant as wax blossoms.

Light treetops its way toward whiter light
that noons ascension via sleek firm wings.

Drops Her Consonants

Drops her consonants I fear
she is weak, mouth too far
open, vulnerable,
I would prefer she firmed

would rather she
crispened each syllable
that others might not
interrupt, edge in

to her universe
that she might be whole
a moment versus
written off I feel responsible

let's say for her
not to be
this pale taken
for granted slip of a girl

I Told Her

I told her sunlight hurt

I told her avert your eyes

I told her tiny parables will rise

I told her vertical indifference of the yurt

I told her innocence makes playthings blond

I told her avenidas long to be intruded on

I told her apertures made flutes whole

I told her venturing would repair forgetfulness

I told her aptitude was rivered in from counties with no name

I told her repertoires are made of golden milk

I told her voice lessons made skin venerable

I told her ice cakes come to light

I told her in my diary midnight shifts the vault of thinking

I told her sleep reverts to day books sunning in the yard unseen

Search and Replace

If you love certainty
do not breathe
a word of it

Say instead that you prefer
to jump from
unreasonable plateaus

Exclaim you only live
once a fiction
makes life shorter

Earns invisible points
makes you kingly
or some such mistake

Tell the crowd you'd rather
Die than know routine
Much less embrace predictability

At all costs
Stay out of your own lane
Put on your fastest running shoes

And trampoline to
mountain height
no one can catch you

Theme and Inequivalencies

Remunerative anger dazzles poverty. *Are you still awake?*
Ventilation whispers evanescence.

Smoke was how I found you. Now in the same place free of
an autumnal fragrance people stand partly gone. And in my
soul, the threat of winter dreams itself.

I play a character immune to cold. I think that walks across
Kalamazoo in subzero weather formed a way of breathing in
a room as if forever were a way of trancing past.

I ask of you these few things I dabble in invention as the
center line allows a fresh new look at how advancement
hastens depth perception inequivalent to death.

To say the word is to recite its antonym. Speaking of leading
I do not. And in your dowry, mention that. Remain immune
or dry your hands or fasten onto punctuation in the form of
a repeated barking of a car a half block from this keyboard.

Ratcheting up expense within the psyche. Mine I have
exhausted every Pinch of sleep and now the waking
breaststroke seeks Its own level meaning liquid I would
navigate as if to see the world.

This

I cannot get the poem out of me.
I cannot get the poem into me.
It is harsh darkness even beneath
the desert sky.

I move numb limbs too fast
and people call that energy.
I have a name for what I do,
and it transcends what I am called.

Is there a calling in desire?
I treat the future like a lover I am quietly
becoming.
How breath comes down to clear

What holds from the moment
long believed to form
a history to revive
the thought of any more.

Portrait without Winter

This is you about to climb into a frame. Consider the observer capable of changing what she sees may shift the way you are remembered. A squadron of protectors litters the museums, keeping artwork safe. Distinguishing possessions from their spirit. Ivy crawls along the brick until no brick is visible. The distance rescues you from thought. Imbalance takes away specifics from informal shadow.

Intonation that approaches touch, how feasible the falling flakes of snow in isolation of collective fact

All About Me

I decided they were tired of hearing so refused to call.
I told myself that they were takers anyway, there was no need
to hitch our stories cluttering past tense. I taught myself
subtraction until mastery overtook my sense of self. Desire to
separate replaced the will to blend. I thought about the icicles
along the eaves. Took up informal geometry as my plaything in
the winter hours.

Distance as repertoire, a melody of comfort as the darkness
placed itself

she practiced
numbness
until it felt
contagious

she rode the bus to see
beautiful beads in polished
hair pulled taut across
competing windows

Separation Envy

You ask me to give back
the aphrodisiac in favor of perfume.
I witness nothing spooned,
I hold the moon in high esteem.
I replicate cuisine I have been cured of needing.
Now is high time to redeem the skin
of being fed to linger past the seed.
Revocable bliss may sprout new selves
and bless the mood trapped within
day-glow happiness about to be bled young.
An overarching speech made sudden
splits into unequal code meant to divide
and alter late-term individuality
as though a serial indifference rose
to the plateau of jaundiced whole.

Hypothesis

He mentioned having a life, perhaps the stillness of a manor
where the people pay a little to lie down and pray the moon
into completion. Or the integers she used to fray to make a
living as she did. Or stars against the strong lean wooden
beam we noticed more than watched. How is it he could
sanctify by merely breathing. I had a father who could fuel
the town with confidence. I had a mother who could warm.
And any incident might be erased for our good and the good
of all our neighbors if they watched. Or ever learned. A
sequel to the shade we sought to reach, as if a culture of
indifference might stand the test of tempo. Anymore, the
faculty of memory subsides into indifference, and the soft
swoon of a written text would blunt the seeming mood.

Overture, a lark, a seam, the sense of sight

Caesura

He teaches me my thinking. I await the fuel, press forward
as his eyes rekindle something not yet said that might be
left alone. That I might answer, offer, change. A little bit like
breathing, each one doing each thing independently. You
never know the chemistry enough. It means the snow is
coming, or it means the shape of any intersection may
adjust to earth as we define. One moment speech, the next
a signal of infatuation. Ramshackle structures, palaces, ripe
peach hues along the beach. Or woodsy fragrance left to be.
I want to learn to center music on the page. I want to hear
the grace tones limber who we are. I want to ask him how
to let me spritz toward winter everywhere. As though
he knows.

Sack cloth, spiritual evidence, some inkling, the perpetual
blank stage

Emphasis

Watch the tree become
the taller tree. Allow
each branch to bear
and loosen leaves
to dust the ground.
Once light arrives,
awake time broadens
to absolve the mind of dream,
recall the way routine
revolves around
routine. And the terrain
as we allow it
shifts mind
to a still place.
The point of finding
anywhere beyond
this a cappella line
of code, an ode
to distillation
or redress or
synthesis as if
the present tense repaired
what we have sought
before it's morphed
and shadowed whole.

It Was Always New

And then nothing
could be lifted
no matter the muscle
or the will

The ground was all
and recollection maybe
feathered any softness
left to be imagined

Again as any number
of defeats were multiplied
times themselves now
fastened down and seen

And felt as though
no sky were ever here
for the duration
I had lived for

Fourteen Lines

I cry fluently in your language
I cloister modesty as if it were reciprocal
I leave work in my psyche constantly undone
I limit fingerings to the literature of the flute
I remain a fixture amid a cappella fortunes
I pay per frugal integer renouncing waste
I limit my enjoyment to deciduous remainders
I pay taxes to the tune of homely homonyms
I retrace your steps and dance in them
I translate slippers into languages of the classics
I tempt Greek and Latin in my sleep
I herald quietude in visual dimensions
I search and replace continents with states of mind
I applaud contingent acts of God for being archetypes

Routinely I Misread You That I Might Invent a Self that Fits

Back when light was raw, I trespassed on your aura.
That was then and made for evening as it landed,
as it spaced apart our twinned intentions separate from
the sprawling situations that returned like copper,

We would warm ourselves and each amid unlikely fabric
like bamboo that did not scratch, just as wool became
so technical you'd think it's cotton,
for the ravishing good times we claimed and claim again,

As though sufficient youth were played against
the odds of flowering or just returning to the mood
we wintered through in seeming youth
with larger numbers near descriptive passages.

How is it still difficult to enact our sun sign
when a painter's all we have become, each one of us.
I told my friend that seeing her resembled learning
that a deity had been there when I thought that none existed.

Now I know, I know the trees are wizened and the line of code
that makes me want to cradle you can be misread.
Routinely I misread you that I may invent a self that fits.
I used to be accused of music in my speech and soul.

A shame that blunted spirit meant that when I spoke to him
I had to hold my shoulders close, that I might protect
the center of a muscular commitment
to what I would be and am and will remain.

There are constant reasons to give up, I read people, picture my mentor
who said never that; the guru now says never that, stay whole.
Are chance procedures relevant, how likely is the yield I see?
It does not matter there is darkness, I retrieve it and I weave,

As though it were enough to know that any raw material
can be transformed, given time and tricks amid the teetering effects
of an unreasoned faith. What matters most is my intention
and what means the least is what a person I have focused on believes.

I used to find it frightening if my love source felt despair.
Now no longer is the sky dependent on adoring fans. It's still the sky.
And minus signs galore have not the power to retract its being.
I am still that sky.

In the New Year

Winter has no sound, a petal fallen on new snow.
Daylight, simple as a noun, comes true again, again.
The quiet of our lives begins
to speak for us, alone, together, strong,

translating even sadness
into fresh biography, sung
by boy sopranos,
pure, specific, virtuosic,

as though there were no world
to chafe the sine wave
that ghosts a center star
to guide our shared lifetimes.

Plaintext

she's soft in her soft clothes and it is Thursday constantly

The mountain dulcimer Louise is fluent on, the lovely fingers of Louise in speech

Once the smoke stopped curling, she could breathe the color of her hair

Recursive wool, uncensored weeds, the river's liberation

Her silence, only slightly noisier than dust

Butterfly brevity, the makeshift in-town lullaby of June

Agnes, dry your hands before approaching fresh new clay

Seeds do not announce themselves, the needed land and rain appear

Nature once so private I believed the leaf required my voice

Skip stones, intone the thought of placid water to be crossed

Bernadean, word of my heart, the bluest of blue eyes, magnetic peace

Shooting baskets in the driveway, summer's permanence

Pines for miles, a drive sans destination

Bivouac, stray soul awaiting a real life

Sad plump young face, harsh curls, in sketch

Held captive by desire to keep her from unhappiness I can't subtract

I hear she is expecting, we are all expecting, sky remains the sky

Stay here with me and within hearing touch that I may breathe again

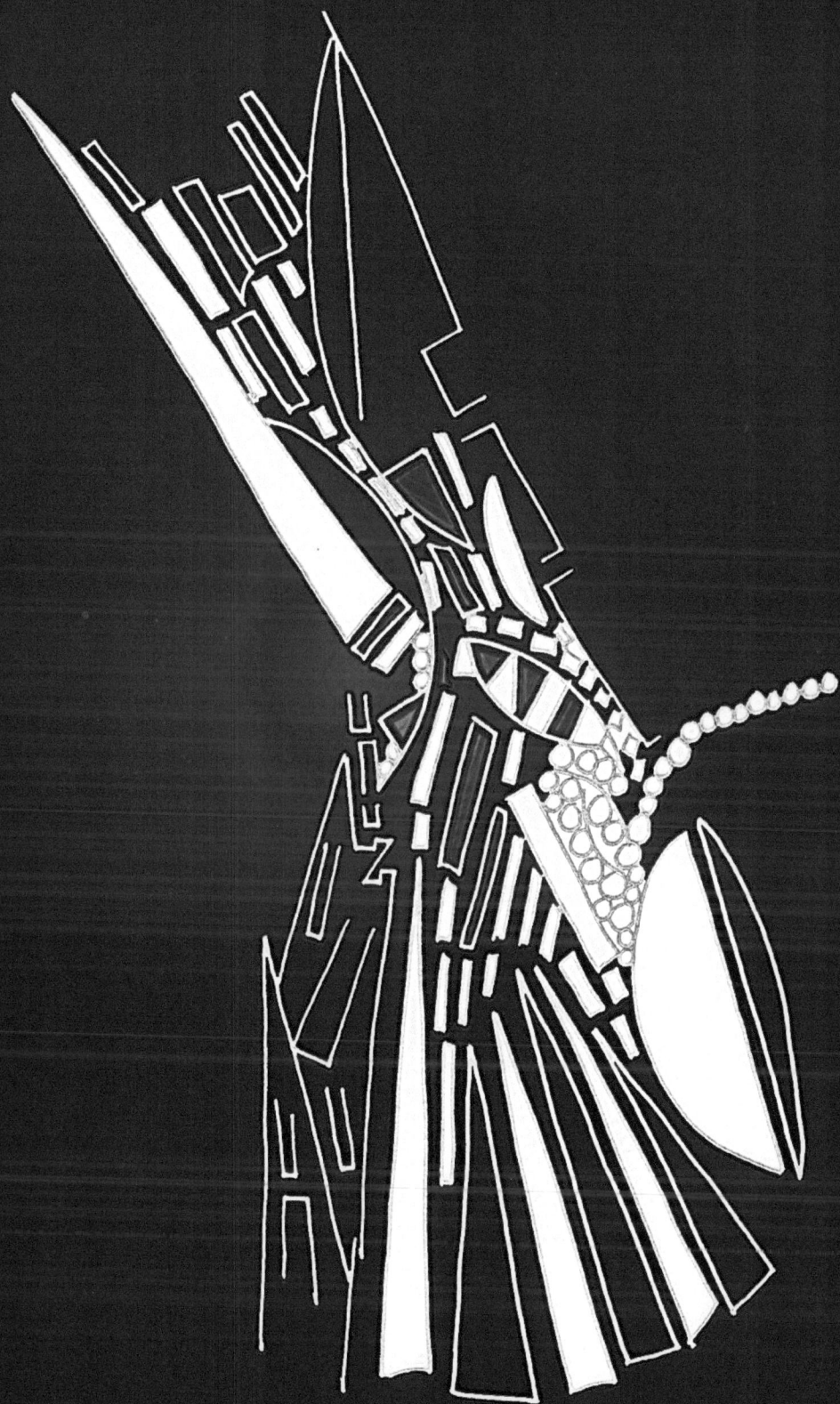

www.ingramcontent.com/pod-product-compliance
Lightning Source LLC
Chambersburg PA
CBHW042042090426
42733CB00027B/49

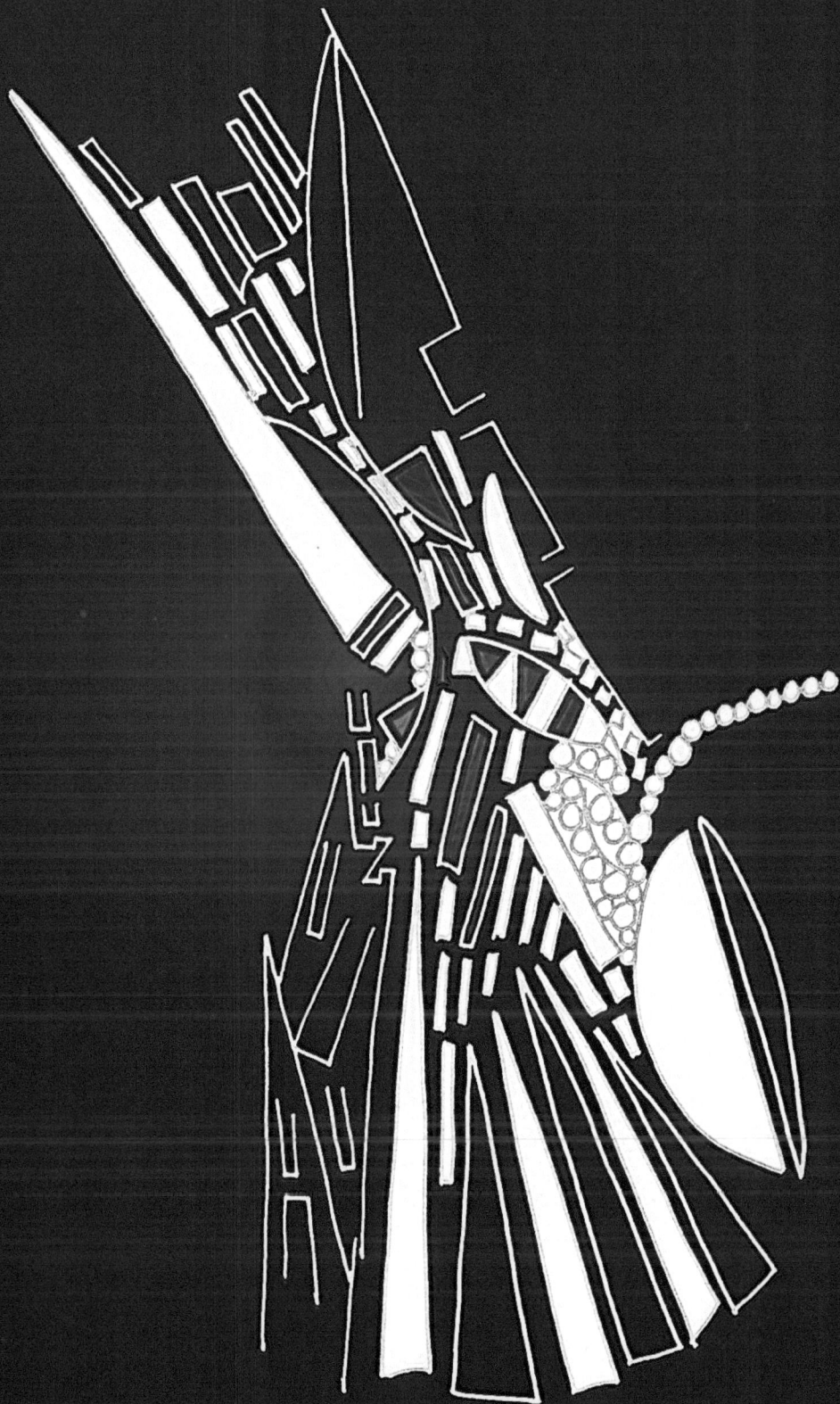